Russia

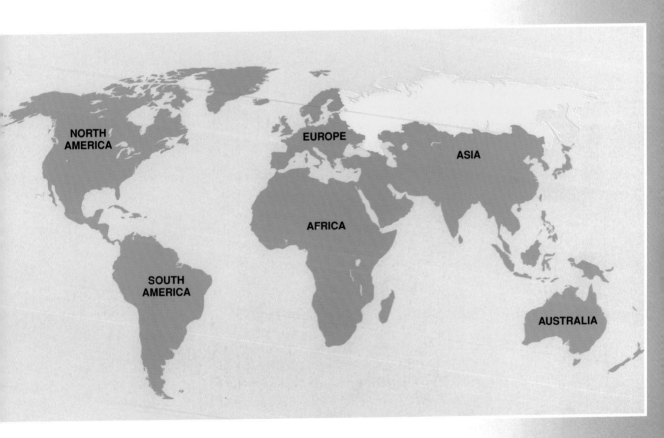

NORTH AMERICA

EUROPE

ASIA

AFRICA

SOUTH AMERICA

AUSTRALIA

Clare Boast

Heinemann Interactive Library
Des Plaines, Illinois

© 1998 Reed Educational & Professional Publishing

Published by Heinemann Interactive Library,
an imprint of Reed Educational & Professional Publishing,
1350 East Touhy Avenue, Suit 240 West, Des Plaines, IL 60018

Produced by Times Offset (M) Sdn. Bhd.
Designed by AMR
Illustrations by Art Construction

02 01 00 99 98
10 9 8 7 6 5 4 3 2 1

Boast, Clare, 1965–
    Russia / Clare Boast
        p.   cm.– – (Next stop!)
    Includes bibliographical references and index.
    Summary: An introduction to the history, geography, culture, and modern daily life in Russia.
    ISBN 1-57572-569-X
    1. Russia (Federation) – –   [1. Russia (Federation)]   I. Title.
II. Series.   97-16745
DK510. 23. B63 1997   C IP
947 – – dc21   AC

Acknowledgments

The author and publisher are grateful to the following for permission to reproduce copyright photographs:
J. Allan Cash Ltd p.28; Colorific! D. Kampfner p.18, P. Turnley p.15; Robert Harding Picture Library P. Van Riel p.24, J. Shakespear p.29; Trip N. Gyngazov p.20, J. Heath p.23, M. Jenkin pp.4, 27, V. Kolpakov p.26, A. Kuznetsov p.9, V. Larionov p.22, N. Rudakov p.8, V. Sidoropolev p.14, A. Tjany-Rjadno pp.7, 12, 13, 16, 17, 19, 21, 25, B. Turner pp.5, 6, N. & J. Wiseman pp.10, 11.

Cover photograph reproduced with permission of Zefa Picture Library/Raga.

Special thanks to Betty Root for her comments in the preparation of this book.

Words in the book in bold, **like this**, are explained in the glossary on page 31.

CONTENTS

INTRODUCTION

St. Basil's Cathedral in Moscow. It was finished in 1560 and is a big **tourist** attraction.

WHERE IS RUSSIA?

Russia stretches east from Europe until it almost touches Alaska. It is a huge country. If you cross Russia, you cross 11 time zones.

Russia has borders with many other countries, from Finland to China. It has many seas around its coastlines.

Communist Russia was made up of more than 100 countries, each with its own language.

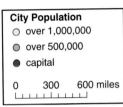

City Population
- ○ over 1,000,000
- ⊙ over 500,000
- ● capital

0   300   600 miles

RUSSIA'S HISTORY

Russia used to be ruled by czars, who were like kings. In 1917, a **revolution** replaced the czars with a **communist government**, and Russia was renamed the USSR. In 1991 the USSR split up. The biggest new country is the Russian Federation.

The Russian flag changed as governments changed. This is the new flag.

THE LAND

Height in feet

- over 3,000
- 1,500–3,000
- 600–1,500
- 0–600

0   300   600
miles

ARCTIC OCEAN

PACIFIC OCEAN

RUSSIA

Kamchatka Peninsula

Volga River

Yenisey River

Lena River

Black Sea

Mt. Elbrus
▲18,510

Caucasus Mountains

Caspian Sea

Lake Baikal

MOUNTAINS

Russia has lots of mountains.
The highest mountains are the
Caucasus Mountains, in the west.
There are many **volcanoes** in the
east of the country. Many of them
still **erupt**.

One of the 22
active volcanoes
in eastern Russia.
One of them has
erupted more
than 70 times
since 1967.

A bridge across the widest part of the Volga River. The Volga is the longest river in Russia.

THE STEPPES

The Steppes is a large, flat plain in southern Russia. The soil here is good for growing crops, and it is easy to use farm machinery on the flat land.

RIVERS AND LAKES

Russia has some of the longest, widest rivers in the world. Most of these rivers flow north to the Arctic Ocean.

There are many lakes in Russia. Some of them, like Lake Balaton in the warm south, have become vacation resorts. Lake Baikal, in Siberia, is too cold for that. But it is the deepest lake in the world.

The Volga River flows into the Caspian Sea. This is not a sea at all, but the largest lake in the world.

7

WEATHER, PLANTS, AND ANIMALS

Murmansk is in the far north of Russia. In December and January, the sun never rises. The temperature is below freezing for half of the year.

THE WEATHER

Russia is so big that there are places where the temperature hardly ever gets above freezing and places where it is so hot it is almost a **desert**.

The size of Russia is one reason for the difference. The other reason is that northern Russia is so far north that the sun, even in summer, is so low in the sky that it doesn't really warm the ground.

PLANTS AND ANIMALS

The far north of Russia has tundra where only moss and small plants can grow in the cold. Polar bears and reindeer live there.

South of the tundra is the taiga—a huge forest of **coniferous** trees. Bears, wolves, and elk live here. South of this, oak and birch trees grow, and there are wild boars and mink. Then there is a high, flat area once covered in grasses. These are the steppes, where polecats live. The areas farthest south are hot and dry.

There are a few tigers in Siberia. But they are hunted for their skins and are dying out.

The taiga is a huge forest that stretches across Russia. The trees are cut down and taken to lumber mills.

TOWNS AND CITIES

Many tourists come to visit St. Petersburg each year. They come to look at the beautiful old buildings and canals.

In 1900, one out of every four people in Russia lived in towns and cities. Now it is three out of every four.

ST. PETERSBURG

St. Petersburg is the second largest city in Russia. It used to be the capital city, until 1918. It was built in 1703 by Czar Peter the Great. It is an important port.

The names of some Russian towns and cities, even streets and squares, have been changed since 1991.

MOSCOW

Moscow became the capital city of Russia in 1918. Moscow has an old center, but has many new offices, factories, and apartment buildings, too. Red Square is in the center of the city. It is called this because the Russian words for "red" and "beautiful" are the same.

FACTORY TOWNS

Many new towns in Russia were built for people who work in the coal, oil, iron, and steel businesses. There are also **nuclear power** plants. Many of these cities create air and water **pollution**.

Most people in Moscow live in small apartments in new high-rise buildings like these. They all look the same.

11

LIVING IN MOSCOW

THE OSHUROV FAMILY

Anatoly and Marina Oshurov live in an apartment in Moscow. They have one girl, Anita, who is twelve.

Anatoly works for a company that sells fruit juice and milk. He works on a computer.

THE FAMILY'S DAY

Anatoly and Marina work full-time. Anita goes to school. Marina works for a company that helps people to leave Russia and move to other countries. Before 1991, it was hard for people to leave Russia. Now it is easier.

The family lives on the top floor of this building. There is no elevator. They have to use the stairs.

MEALTIMES

The family eats together most evenings.
They like beet soup, pancakes, and salad.
They try to eat balanced meals with
meat and vegetables, but food is
expensive and there is not much choice.
The family spends a lot of time shopping.
There are often long lines. They go to
local stores and markets.

Anita's classroom at school. There is homework every night.

The apartment
is very small.
The family eats
in the kitchen.

FARMING IN RUSSIA

These machines are harvesting wheat. Only big, government-run farms can buy machines like this.

GROWING WHEAT

Wheat grows well on the flat steppes. The soil and the weather are good. The land is flat, so farmers can use big machines to plow the soil and cut the wheat. But sometimes the farmers cannot grow enough to feed all the people, so there are food shortages.

GOVERNMENT FARMS

Before 1991, the **government** ran all the farms. They chose what to grow and what prices to charge. The government still owns most big farms, which grow wheat, barley, oats, and potatoes.

OTHER FARMS

Now farmers can run their own farms. They are mostly small and near towns. Usually, they grow vegetables and fruit to sell in the local market.

Only 14 percent of the land is good for farming. The rest is too cold or steep, or is already built on.

Soldiers help pick potatoes on a government-run farm.

LIVING IN THE COUNTRY

The house is bigger than an apartment in the city. It has five rooms. They have a TV, a stereo, and a washing machine.

THE DMITREIEV FAMILY

Sergey and Olga Dmitreiev live in a village in the southwest of Russia. They have one boy, Andrey, who is nine, and one girl, Misha, who is two. In the village, everyone works on the same farm.

The villagers do most of their own repair work on the farm machines.

THE FAMILY'S DAY

Sergey plows the soil or drives the harvester. Olga looks after the cows. Andrey goes to school in the village.

Olga helps Andrey with his homework in the evenings.

EARNING A BIT MORE

The family has a garden where they grow cabbages, tomatoes, cucumbers, beets, and apples. If they grow more than they can eat, they sell it to other villagers.

MEALTIMES

The family eats breakfast together in the morning. They eat their main meal in the evening. Sergey and Olga grow a lot of the vegetables they need. They can buy bread and meat at stores in the village.

RUSSIAN STORES

CHANGING TIMES

Before 1991, the **communist government** ran the stores. They sold basic foods, like bread and potatoes, at a set price. There were often long lines. It was hard to get things like clothes and shoes.

Now anyone can open a store and set their own prices. There are more things to buy, but very few people can afford them.

A new shopping center. Only wealthy people, like the woman here, can afford to buy things in these stores.

In Russian stores you pay first. You get a ticket for the things you want. Then you trade the ticket for the things you have paid for.

MARKETS

There are street markets all over Russia. They are often the only places where you can buy fruit and vegetables.

Farmers, who grow more than they need, sell the food to passing customers. Because there are often food shortages, people who have food to sell can charge a lot of money.

*Some stores, especially those selling things to **tourists**, do not take Russian money. They ask to be paid in foreign money, like U.S. dollars.*

RUSSIAN FOOD

These people have wrapped up warm for a barbecue. This is as hot as the weather gets!

TRADITIONAL FOOD

Russia has many traditional foods, because it has many cultures. Borsch (beet soup), blinis (pancakes), tabaka (chicken with cabbage and prunes), and stroganoff (beef with onion, mushrooms, and sour cream) are all traditional foods.

Many adults in Russia drink vodka. It is an alcoholic drink made from potatoes and is very cheap.

ORDINARY FOOD AND DRINKS

Most people cook with what they can find in the stores and markets. They change recipes to fit what they find. They drink mostly black tea and vodka.

SPECIAL FOOD AND DRINKS

Not much Russian food is sold to other countries. But Russian vodka is sold all over the world. Most of the caviar from Russia is sold to other countries. Caviar is made of very expensive fish eggs.

This family is eating soup, bread, and vegetables from their garden, with spicy sausages.

MADE IN RUSSIA

These tractors will be used by lumberjacks to cut down and saw up trees that will then be sold to other countries.

Russia is starting to sell more **exports** to other countries. Russia did not export much at all before 1991.

FACTORIES

Before 1991, factories had to make what the **government** told them to. They made tanks, tractors, railroad freight cars, ships, and also things like shoes and furniture.

Russia mines more gold than any other country in the world.

Factories, like this metal factory, create a lot of air and water pollution. Piles of waste material build up, too.

CHANGES

Since 1991, the government has tried to change what factories make. They want them to make washing machines and microwaves, not tanks. They also want them to be more careful about **pollution**.

The government wants factories to make things for export. This will make money for Russia. They will be able to sell the export **goods** at cheaper prices, because workers in Russia earn less than workers in most other countries in Europe.

GETTING AROUND

Irkutsk station. Most people travel or send goods long distances by train, not road.

Travel in Russia can be a problem. Long distances and bad weather cause delays.

TRAINS

You can travel across Russia on the Trans-Siberian railroad. There are smaller railroad lines all across the country.

ROADS

The best roads in Russia are in the west of the country, linking Moscow and other cities like St. Petersburg. Many roads in the rest of Russia are gravel or dirt and are often blocked with snow.

In the Siberian winter, the rivers freeze so hard that drivers use them as roads when the roads are blocked by snow!

CITY TRAVEL

It is easier to travel in the cities than outside them. Most cities have good **public transportation**, because only a few people own cars. Buses and subways are cheap and quick. With less traffic, there is less **pollution**.

Moscow subway stations have all been decorated in different ways. This one looks very grand. Others look very modern.

SPORTS AND VACATIONS

SPORTS

Russian sports training is very good. They have good soccer and ice hockey teams. Russian athletes often do well at the Olympic Games.

Most Russian cities have sports fields, swimming pools, and ice rinks that are cheap to use.

Now that Russia is making more links with other countries, sports like tennis and golf are becoming popular. But they are expensive, and there are not many places to play.

Reindeer racing is popular in Murmansk, in the north of Russia.

This dacha, weekend home, is very fancy. Most dachas are not decorated like this.

TIME OFF

City people often stay with relatives in the country on weekends. Some people have their own dachas. Most dachas are small wooden houses with tiny gardens.

VACATIONS

Only a few Russians can afford to go to other countries for vacations. Mostly, they go to different parts of Russia. They may go to the north for skiing or to a hot vacation resort in the south.

FESTIVALS AND ARTS

Priests from the Russian Orthodox Church celebrate Easter. This public celebration could not have happened under communist rule.

RELIGIOUS FESTIVALS

The **communist government** did not believe in religion. The Russian Orthodox Church had to hold its services in secret. People now celebrate these festivals again.

OTHER FESTIVALS

The biggest nonreligious festival is held on May 1st. It is International Solidarity Day. It celebrates the contributions of Russian workers.

The Russian State Library in Moscow has more than 30 million books.

ARTS

Russia has many museums, art galleries, and theaters. Russian art will become more well-known as Russia has more and more contact with other countries.

Russian music and ballet are already famous. The Moscow State Circus performs all over the world. There are many circuses that travel all over Russia.

This parade celebrates the end of World War II. The parade is held on May 9th every year.

RUSSIA FACT FILE

People
People from Russia are called Russians.

Capital city
The capital city is Moscow.

Largest cities
Moscow is the largest city. Nearly 9 million people live in Moscow. St. Petersburg is the second largest city, and Nizhniy Novgorod is the third largest.

Head of country
The head of Russia is called the president.

Population
There are about 150 million people living in Russia.

Money
People use rubles and kopecks. 1 ruble = 100 kopecks

Language
Most people speak Russian but some speak Tartar, Ukrainian, Chuvash, or other Russian languages.

Religion
The most common religions in Russia are Christianity, Islam, and Buddhism.

MORE BOOKS TO READ

Flint, David. *Russia*. Austin, TX: Raintree Steck-Vaughn, 1993.
Perrin, Penelope. *Russia*. Morristown, NJ: Silver Burdett Press, 1994.

GLOSSARY

canals These are manmade waterways.

communist This describes someone who believes everything—work, land, money—should be shared out equally between everyone.

coniferous forest This is a forest of trees that keep their leaves all year round.

desert This is a hot dry place with little water where hardly anything can grow.

erupt This is when a volcano throws out ash and lava.

exports These are things that are sold to other countries.

goods These are things people make.

government This is the people who run the country.

nuclear power This is energy that can be used to make electricity by using nuclear reactions.

plain This is a large flat area of land.

pollution This is dirt in the air, water, or on land.

public transportation This means buses, taxis, or trains that can be used by anyone who can pay the fare.

revolution This is when the people in a country fight to get rid of their rulers.

tourist Someone who visits a place on vacation.

volcano This is a mountain that sometimes throws out ash and melted rock.